The Glasgow Survival Guide

Written by:	Jamie Simpson
Doodles:	Thomas Wright
Edited by:	Mark Hilferty
Assistance by:	Paul Martin

For my boy, Jack.

I moved to Glasgow from the Highlands of Scotland in 2007.

I always knew life would be different in the city, but I wasn't quite prepared for just how different.

The pace of life here is lightning quick, the scale of buildings and volume of people is breath-taking, however, the most mind-blowing difference is their use of language.

The Glasgow Survival Guide was started on Twitter where I share some observations from my day-to-day.

Here are just a few tips on how to survive in the 'Big Smoke'.

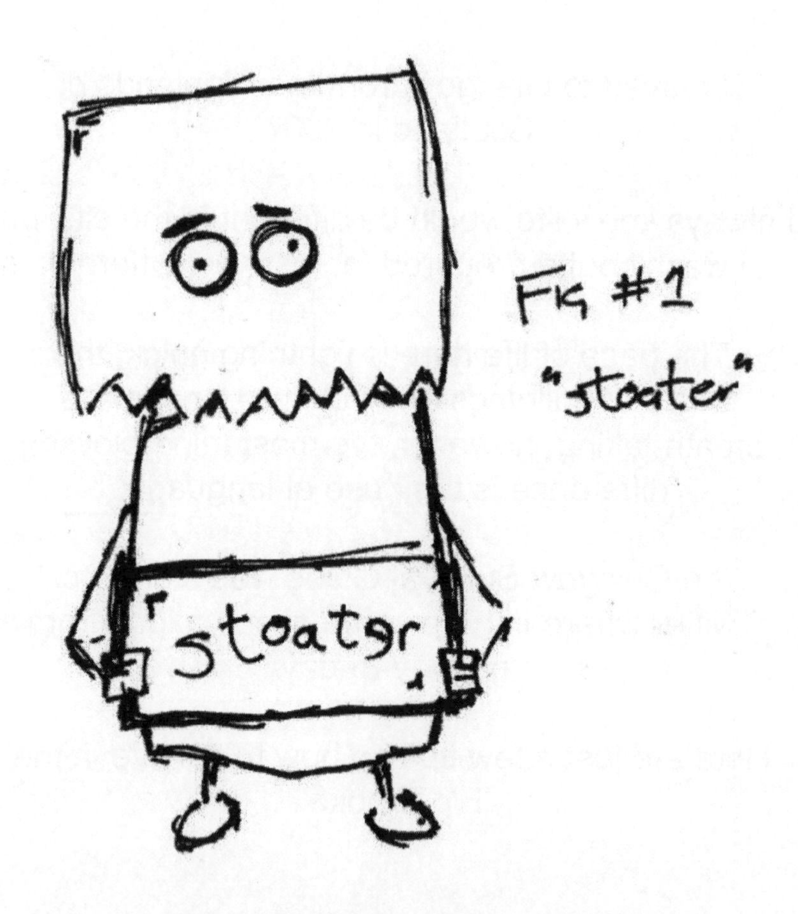

'Stoat' has many forms both good and bad.
You can be a real 'stoater'
Although this is often used in sarcasm.

"Aye, a right stoater!"

My name is 'Big man', or so it seems.

Your name is very much determined by your height.

I'm 6ft 4 inches, so in Glasgow, I'm taller than most.

From buying the newspaper in the morning to passing my neighbour in the evening.

"Alright, Big man?"

"How you doing, Big man?"

"You got a spare 50p, Big man?"

Better than 'Wee man', I guess.

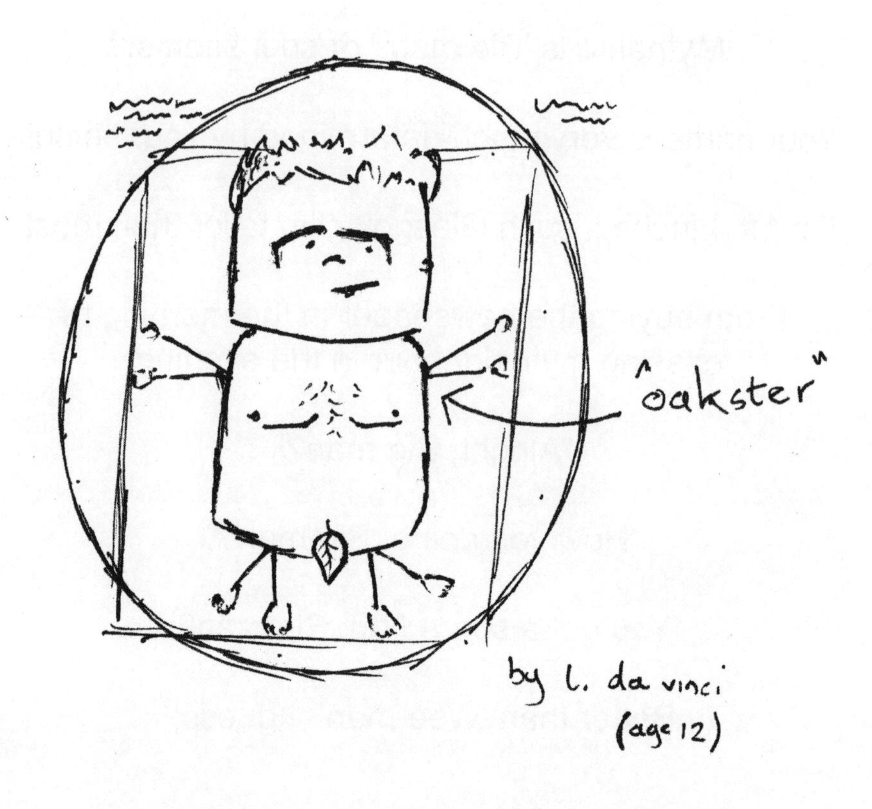

Glaswegians even have body parts that all other humans do not…

"Yer oaxter!"

Weight is such a funny topic in Glasgow.

If you want to emphasise anything you can preface it with the word ‘heavy’.

“I was heavy drunk last night.”

“Aww, that was heavy funny.”

“You’re heavy stinking!”

Facelifts come in two forms – one you'll pay thousands for and the other is the cost of a hair bobble.

The Glasgow Facelift.

My first trip to the Barras was a memorable one.

I was wearing a smart black jacket and a pair of jeans.

This might not strike you as something that's unusual, or
would cause me to stand out in the crowd,
but I was wrong.

"Are you the bizzies?"

"Excuse me? Am I the what now?"

"Are you the Polis?"

"Oh. Eh, no, no I'm not."

No tracksuit, no conformity!

Piracy is a crime.

Unless you work in the Barras, then it's just a job.

Nothing is ever flat in this city.

You'll either be "going up to the shoaps" or "doon the road".

Up or doon; those are your only choices!

Someone referring to 'ma bit' or 'ma gaff' is talking about their house.

"Up ma gaff!"

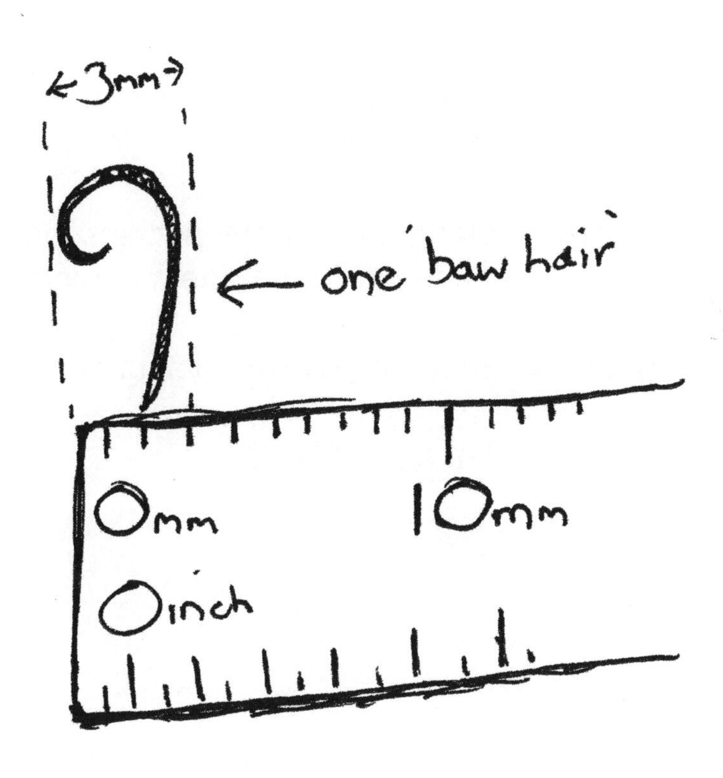

A 'baw hair' is a unit of measurement.

The people of Glasgow can miss things by a 'baw hair'.

Highlanders call it a millimetre.

I'll never forget the first time I was told
to 'haud my wheesht'.

Frantically rummaging through my pockets looking
for my *wheesht* to later learn the meaning:

'haud yer wheesht': (*verb*) "to shut up"

I'm a loud drunk.

A Glaswegian will say “Am away fur a pint”

yet they always seem to come back drunk...

Just how big was the pint?

A ‘nummar-waan’ and a ‘shoart back an-sides’ are names of popular haircuts.

Now I'm sure this isn't strictly a Glasgow thing, but any Highlanders will find this a little strange.

When you walk into a kebab shop, you'll find something that can only have derived from sheep shearing... the kebab shaver!

These gents shave kebab meat off a drum and could make a fortune up in the hills.

Not a woolly sheep in sight.

'Bobby' is most definitely not 'boaby'.

In the same light a 'job' is not a 'jobby'.

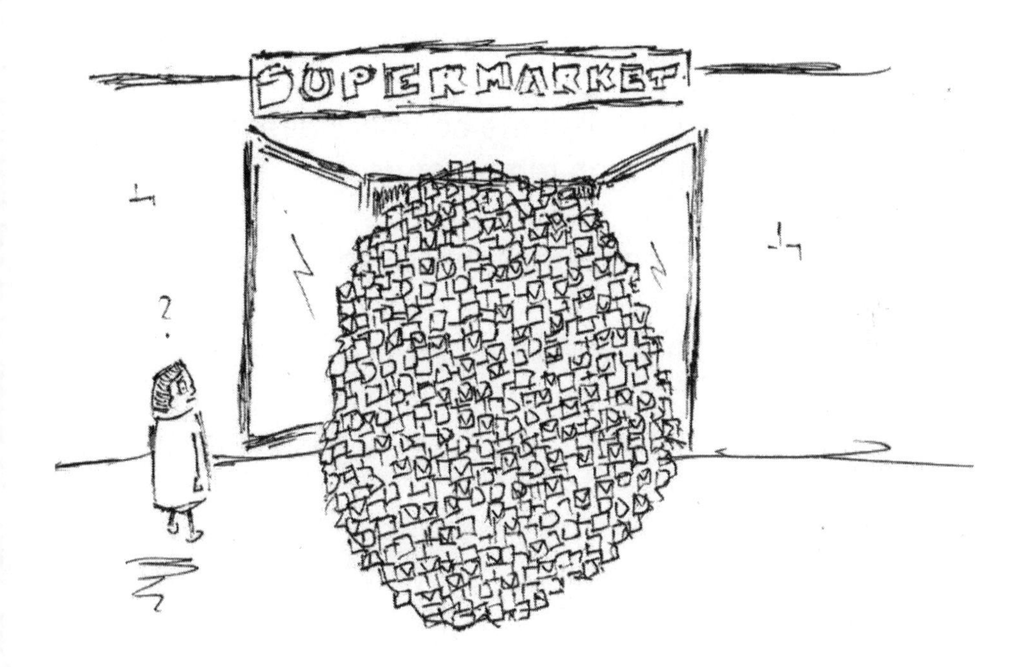

There are more ‘messages’ paid for in a Glasgow Tesco than found in a Royal Mail sorting office.

You'll need to understand how to survive your first trip to Greggs.

The lovely ladies behind the counter have a unique take on temperature.

"Any heat left in that pasty?"

The answer will be one of three:

"Aye, it's ok" – this is your green light, good to go, dive on in.

"There's a wee bit heat left" – rest assured it will be stone cold.

"Aye, there's some heat in it." – prepare for a mouth injury!

Highland night out: pub > mate's house > home.

Glasgow night out: taxi > pub > club > casino > A+E Department.

They really do things a little bit differently down here in the Big Smoke.

This place is so confusing!

The word ‘hanky’ can be misleading.

It’s either a tissue, or a word used to preface ‘panky’ but I’ll not explain what that is, ask your parents.

Kicking back watching a movie when I'm interrupted by two arguing members of the local young team.

If this ever happens to you while you're in Glasgow, pause the movie, open your window and listen.

You'll hear some of the most fascinating use of language.

The first lad started, "Bolt ya rocket, before I launch ye!"

"Naw mate, your patter's like wa'ter"
I later find out this has an ending of 'it runs'.

"Don't you start on ma patter ya wee prick, ma patter's like toothpaste, pure mint't!" as they scurried out of earshot.

Pure magic.

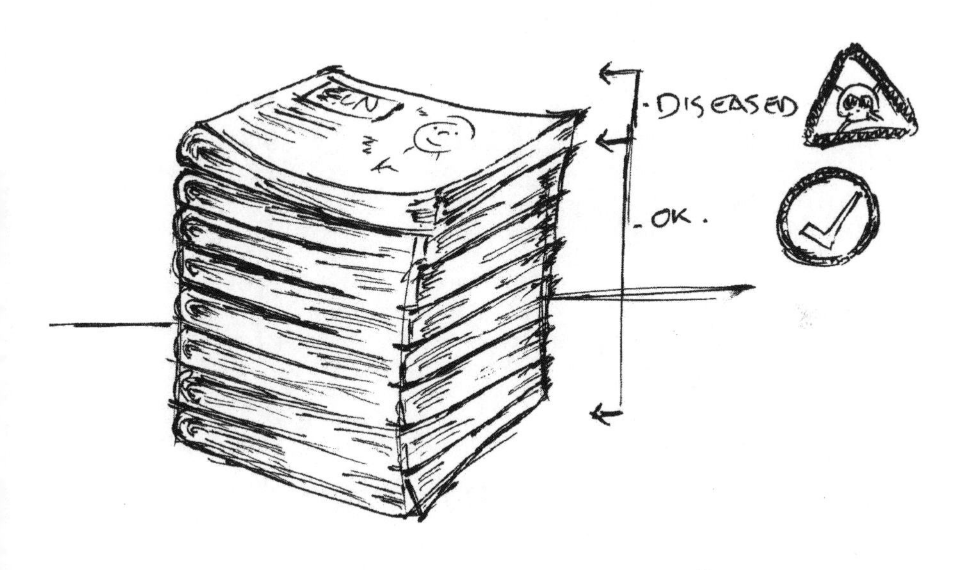

The top newspaper on the pile is diseased.

Well it must be, everyone down here takes the one under it.

Always… like an unwritten rule.

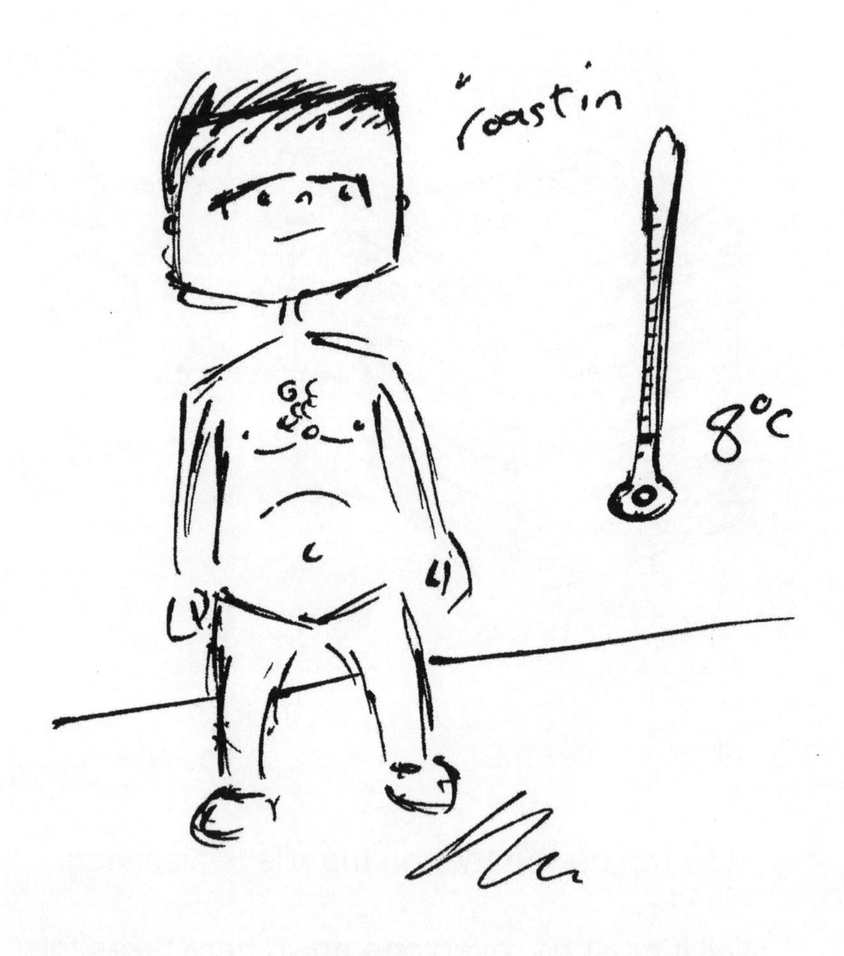

During the ‘summer’ these fine gentlemen have 1 rule.

If you see the sun (even if it’s just partially)
you declare ‘taps aff!’

I've since found out there are more commonly used lines to be invited to battle.

The word 'go' has a shape down here.

"Square go!"

Also known as a 'Square G'.

Then you have the classic schoolboy – "You talking tae me or ye chewin a brick?"

Regardless what you say next, the response will be "Either way you'll be losing some teeth."

Speaking of fighting – ‘moan then’ isn’t an open mic session to gripe about politics or the weather.

Prepare for battle.

In the Highlands we have an ice cream van. It will come round just once a week, and only in the summer months.

Glasgow has a full array of vans all scrambling around the streets on a daily basis.

In one area alone, you'd find two grocery vans, a chip-shop van, a van that sold you some rolls in the morning, one that stopped outside the school to sell hotdogs and even a van selling fish.

You can even buy a single cigarette from the ice cream van if you don't have enough cash to buy a whole pack, they'll even give you a single match.

Doesn't anyone buy anything from a shop down here?

A Glasgow smile isn't something to be happy about.

For weeks I was calling my car a ‘mush’.

I guess that’s what happens when you overhear a conversation and don’t really understand it.

“What’s wrong with your mush?”

“Ach, it’s my exhaust, I’m going to have to replace the whole thing.”

How was I supposed to know they were asking why he was in a mood?

“What’s changed your tune?”

Highlanders, this is not music related.

Your ‘tune’ is your mood.

Catching your first bus in the city is quite the challenge, until you know the rules.

I was standing at the bus stop waiting patiently for my number 62 bus to arrive to take me to work.

I watched the bus approach me but it didn't stop, it just kept going.

At least in the highlands you don't have to flag down your own bus.

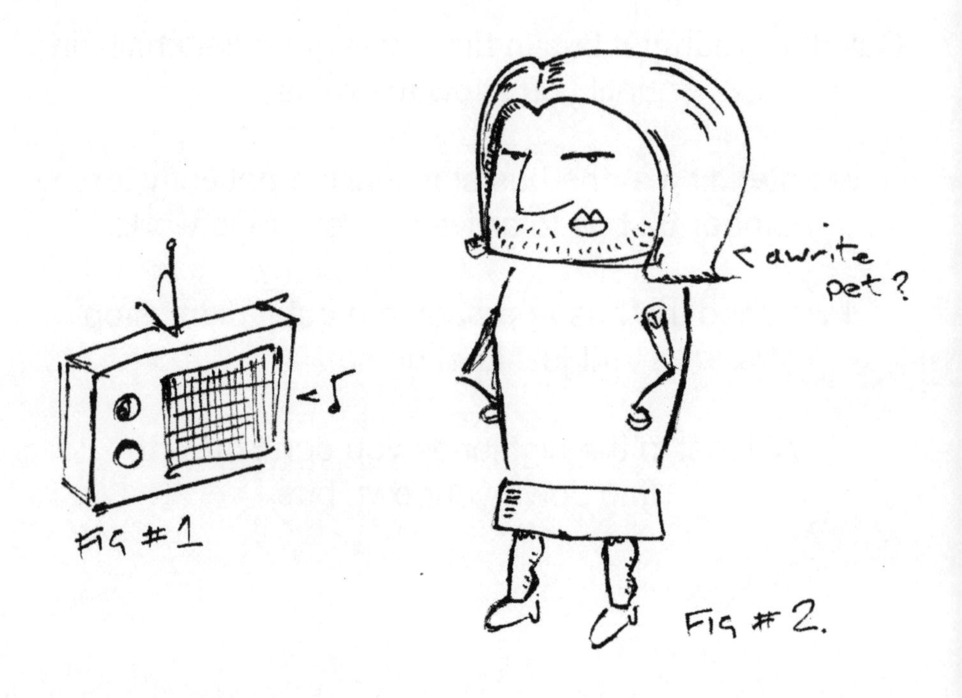

Highlanders, down here you can tune in a tranny.

I know that will sound shocking to you,
but don't worry… it's the radio.

I was sitting back sipping on a cup of tea when I was asked "Did you hear that budgie above the hoose last night?"

I couldn't help but think how big this bird had to be for me to be able to hear it.

"No, but should I be able to hear a budgie flying above the house?"

Everyone fell about laughing; a budgie is another word for a helicopter.

The universal name for everything is 'thingy'.

Asking for the remote control is 'geez that thingy'.

You Highlanders will get the idea.

The thing about cars in Glasgow, it doesn't matter if you drive a 1980's Skoda or a brand new Ferrari, it will always be called your "moaturr".

“Oan yer bike” has nothing to do with cycling.

Ordering a simple drink of juice is an ordeal in this place.

"Do you want some ginger?"

"Some ginger what?"

"Naw, a glass of ginger?"

"...The spice?"

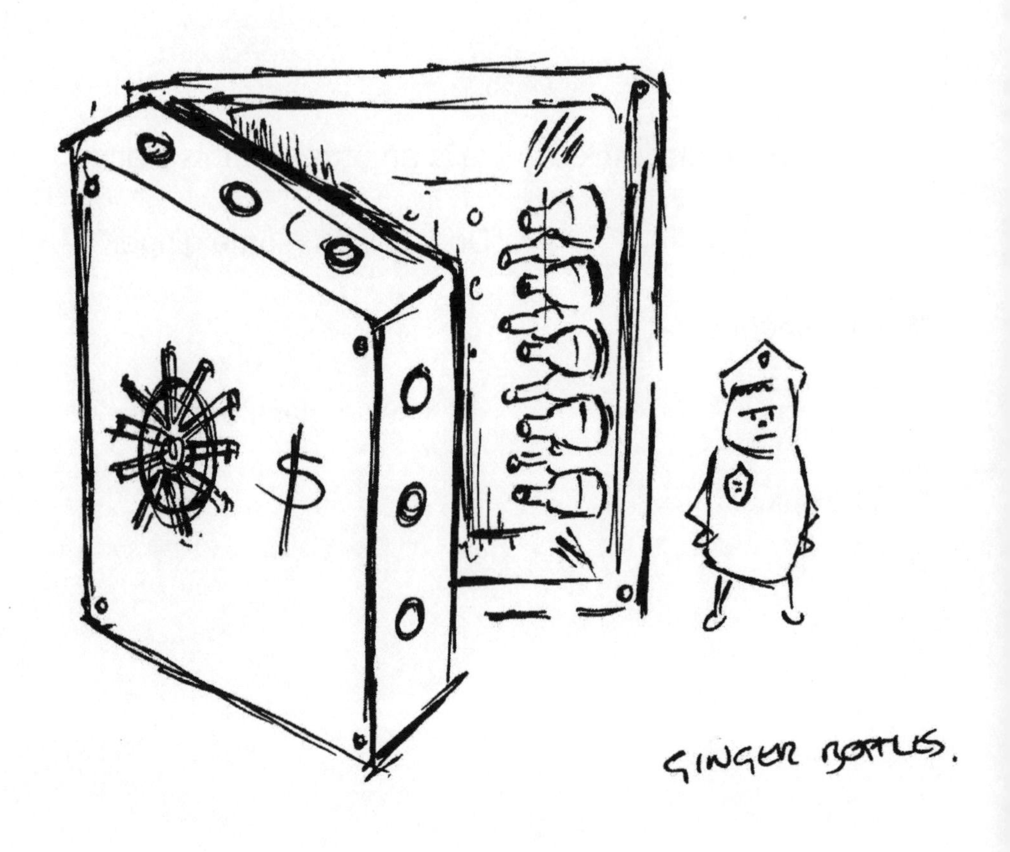

“Gingie boatles” are a form of currency.

Be wary of someone wanting to give you a Glasgow Kiss.

There's an army of women in Glasgow that should be both feared, and avoided, at all costs.

They're kind enough to wear the same uniform though, so you'll easily recognise them.

Look out for the dark orange skin, often found to be wearing pyjamas and like to assemble at bus stops or 24 hour supermarkets.

The elite members of the group can be identified by the cigarette hanging from their mouth and being followed by a small child called Chantelle or Shelby.

Or worse… Henrik or Barry.

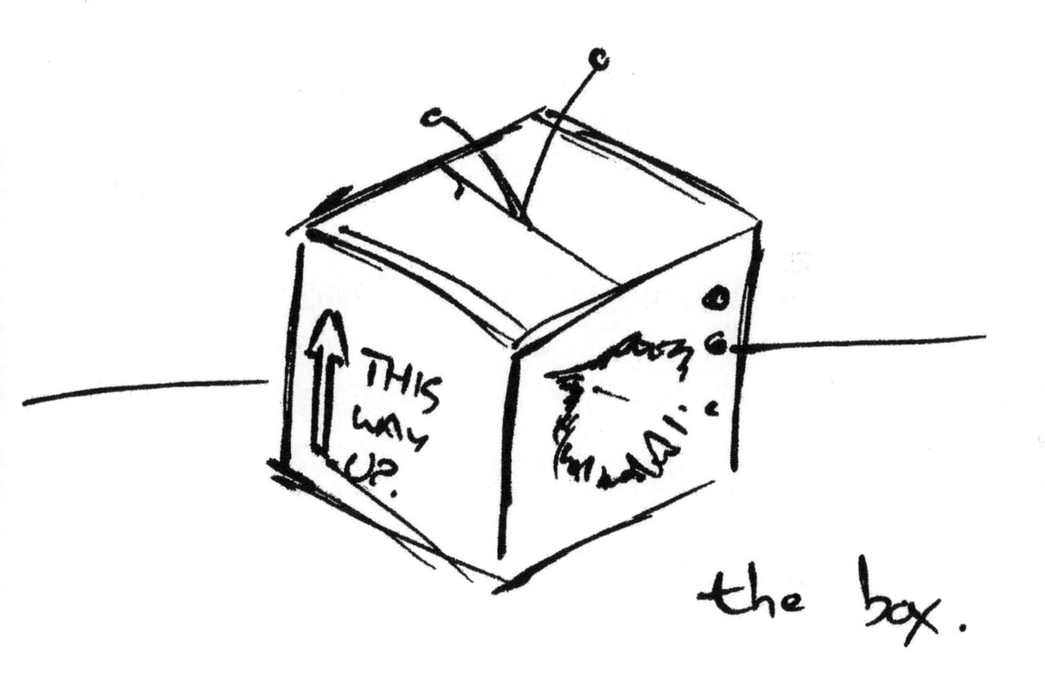

“What’s oan the box tonight?”
Fear not Northerners, the ‘box’ is the TV.

Yeah, you're right; it's just too confusing down here...

I'm going home.

Glossary

A
ach: well
aff: off
aye: yes

B
baw: ball
Big Smoke: big city
bizzies: the police
boatle: bottle
box: television
budgie: helicopter

G
gaff: house
geez: give
ginger: juice or colour
gingie: ginger
Glaswegian: a person from Glasgow

H
hanky: tissue
haud: hold
heavy: really
hoose: house

J
jobby: poop

M
ma: my or mum
messages: shopping
mint't: minted
moan: come-on
moaturr: car
mush: face

N
naw: no
nummar: number

O
oan: on
oaxter: armpit

P
polis: the police

S
shoart: short
stoater: great

T
taps: tops
thingy: thing
tranny: radio
tune: mood

W
wan: one
wa'ter: water
wee: small
wheesh

Thanks to:

Mark Hilferty (for convincing me to go through with this crazy idea); Tommy Wright (for being understanding when it came to my terrible ideas in the doodling department); Paul Martin (for not telling me to go away every single time I approached him for something); The lovely people of Glasgow (for creating what has to be the best city in the world); my amazing Twitter followers (your motivation and encouragement has been incredible) and finally, Lisa Gardiner (for putting up with me during this).

Look out for the future publications of: -

The Highland Survival Guide

and

The Office Survival Guide

Printed in Great Britain
by Amazon.co.uk, Ltd.,
Marston Gate.